The Wondrous Cross

Iain D Campbell

EP BOOKS
Faverdale North
Darlington
DL3 0PH, England

web: www.epbooks.org

e-mail: sales@epbooks.org

EP Books are distributed in the USA by:
JPL Distribution
3741 Linden Avenue Southeast
Grand Rapids, MI 49548
E-mail: orders@jpldistribution.com
Tel: 877.683.6935

British Library Cataloguing in Publication Data available

ISBN 978–1–78397–002–5

Contents

Introduction

There is possibly no composition in the history of English hymnody more loved than Isaac Watt's eighteenth-century classic, 'When I survey the wondrous cross'. One writer says that of all the six hundred or so hymns that Watts wrote, 'none ever equalled the colourful imagery and genuine devotion of this emotionally stirring and magnificent hymn text'.[1]

In her study of English hymn-writers, Faith Cook notes that Isaac Watts was a brilliant scholar, knowledgeable in Latin and of exceptional poetic ability, yet 'he expressed his thoughts in the plain Anglo-Saxon diction of the common man'.[2] That is one of the great appeals of the hymn which is the basis of these studies, which I hope are also in the diction of the common man. In his hymn, Watts does not say everything that might be said about the cross, but he does call our attention to it, and the claims that it makes on those who will study it biblically and sincerely.

The author

Isaac Watts lived from 1674 to 1748. As a young child in Southampton he showed considerable skill in language, studying Latin by the age of 4 and composing poetry by the age of 6. By the time he was a teenager he had already become familiar with French, Greek and Hebrew.

Watts' father was a dissenting minister, who refused to conform to the law of the land regarding the worship of God, and was in prison for his nonconformity when his son Isaac was born. Both the piety and the principles of his father made a lasting impression on him, and he professed faith in Christ at the age of fifteen. Watts spent some time thereafter studying in London, then tutoring the son of an aristocrat.

While a tutor he became associated with Mark Lane Independent Church in London. One of the first things that impacted him was the dull singing; both the use of the psalms in worship as well as the uninspiring way in which they were sung convicted him of the importance of improving the worship and offering God the best. To that end Watts began preaching, writing hymns and encouraging better singing.

Eventually Watts was invited to become an assistant at Mark Lane since the minister was ill. In 1702 he took the position of pastor, although his health was never robust. One biographer says that 'As a pastor, Watts was almost all that could be wished.

He was an orator, and his sermons were invariably fresh, thoughtful and stimulating; indeed, the only complaint the congregation made against him was that they saw too little of him in their homes'.[3]

But his industry in study is evident in the legacy of hymns which he left us. He has been called the 'father of the English hymn',[4] since his was a deliberate attempt to replace old covenant psalms with new covenant hymns. In the preface of one of his works, Watts explains his aim, which was 'to accommodate the book of Psalms to Christian Worship'. With this end in view, he was not in favour of using all the Psalms in Christian worship; but he was in favour of supplementing the Psalms of the Old Testament with Bible-based compositions with an overt evangelical message. Watts wrote:

I am fully satisfied that more honour is done to our blessed Saviour by speaking his name, his graces and actions in his own language, according to the brighter discoveries he has now made, than by going back again to the Jewish forms of worship, and the language of types and figures.[5]

This principle was evident in the publication in 1707 of a collection of Isaac Watts' *Hymns and Spiritual Songs in Three Books, Collected from the Scriptures, Composed on Divine Subjects, Prepared for the Lord's Supper; With an Essay towards the improvement of Christian Psalmody, by the use of evangelical hymns in worship as well as the Psalms of David.*

Psalms, hymns and spiritual songs?

Watts anticipated the controversy that would follow. And it is a controversy that has raged over the last two centuries, so that the language of 'worship wars' is now common in church circles. When churches split, it is rarely over matters of doctrine; it is often over matters of worship.

My own denomination, the Free Church of Scotland, had been committed to the exclusive use of psalms in worship up until a Plenary Assembly decided to mandate the use of evangelical hymns in worship, subject to several conditions. Psalms are still to be used in worship, and the freedom of conscience of church office-bearers is to be respected.

I had argued strongly for the Psalms-only position in our denomination, and would still argue that it is perfectly competent for Christian worship to be offered with the use of the hymns that the Bible itself provides. That was the tradition in which I grew up, and I never thought that my worship was sub-Christian or old covenant. Indeed, in the congregation of which I am pastor, we still sing only the Psalms, in a metrical form. None of which, of course, justifies singing them badly!

Yet even in my Gaelic-speaking tradition I was always aware of the power of verse to express the longings and desires of the Christian life. The singing of hymns was often a part of private and family devotion, even if it was not part of public worship as I experienced it. My exposure to the tradition of English evangelical hymns was enriching and edifying, and I often quote hymns in worship and in preaching.

So I happily sit at the feet of Isaac Watts; and even if I am not entirely convinced by his argument that the new covenant necessitates a new hymnody, I am glad to learn from him, and meditate at the grandeur of the vision expressed in his hymns, as well as the power of the devotional element in them.

I invite you to do the same as we take the best-known of all his hymns as the basis for our studies on the cross of Christ. Composed for a communion service, 'When I survey the wondrous cross' was published in the 1707 collection under the title, 'Crucifixion to the World by the Cross of Christ'. In its original form it had a fourth stanza which is often omitted in current editions. This stanza reads:

> His dying crimson, like a robe,
> Spreads o'er his body on the tree;
> Then am I dead to all the globe,
> And all the globe is dead to me.

The four chapters of this short book were prepared for a communion weekend in the APC Church in Stornoway on the Isle of Lewis in August 2012, another psalm-singing church, which received these messages warmly. Indeed, the presence of the Lord was very evident as we gathered together for worship and to remember the Lord's death.

I trust that these studies will enable us all to gaze in wonder at the cross of Jesus Christ, and discover its power afresh. It is truly the place where the world can be put to death for us, and its true value seen. It is also the place where we can be put to death to the world, and have our lives re-oriented around the things of God. God grant that it may be so, and that we will be able to sing, if not in our churches, then certainly in our hearts, the words from the eighteenth century that resonate with the glorious gospel of a crucified Redeemer:

When I survey the wondrous cross
On which the Prince of Glory died
My richest gain I count but loss
And pour contempt on all my pride.

Forbid it, Lord, that I should boast,
Save in the death of Christ my God,
All the vain things that charm me most,
I sacrifice them to his blood.

See, from his head, his hands, his feet,
Sorrow and love flow mingled down!
Did e'er such love and sorrow meet;
Or thorns compose so rich a crown?

Were the whole realm of nature mine,
That were a present far too small;
Love so amazing, so divine,
Demands my soul, my life, my all.

IAIN D CAMPBELL

September 2012

1

Surveying the cross

And when they had crucified him, they divided his garments among them by casting lots. Then they sat down and kept watch over him there. And over his head they put the charge against him, which read, 'This is Jesus, the King of the Jews.' Matthew *27:35–37*

Behold my Servant Isaiah 42:1

When I survey the wondrous cross
On which the Prince of Glory died
My richest gain I count but loss
And pour contempt on all my pride.

To survey something is to look at it intently, to study it carefully, to examine it minutely. That is what the gospel commands us to do—to pay attention to the cross work of Jesus Christ. Everything Jesus did he did with the cross in view, and with the cross in mind. All his roads would lead him to Calvary. And it is the function of the Gospel to enable us to survey the cross of Jesus.

And it is important to survey the cross for two fundamental reasons.

First, apart from the cross there is no salvation. The gospel makes the cross indispensable. It is the one thing we must have if we are to have our sins forgiven. Most people believe in justification by death; because God is good and loving and kind, he takes everyone to Heaven when they die. On the other side of that veil there is nothing but good for people no matter what their life has been. That is the common perception.

But the gospel comes with a different message. It tells us that we are justified by a death, but not ours. It is not our dying that will bring us to Heaven; but there is a dying that will bring us to Heaven. Access to Heaven is dependent on the dying of another. Our road to Heaven is indirect: we have to go to the cross of Calvary. There is no other way of being saved. No matter what we know, or experience, or offer, we cannot be saved unless we trust to what Jesus did for us on the cross of Calvary. All our hope and confidence is grounded on the cross, and centred in the cross. Truly there is salvation in no-one and in nothing else (Acts 4:12). The name of salvation is emblazoned on a Roman cross.

In other words, if I am unsaved, a stranger to God and his grace, without title to Heaven or hope of eternal life, it is to the cross of Calvary I must come. This is the fountain that God opened for sin and for

uncleanness (Zechariah 13:1). All who enter Heaven—
every last one of the great crowd that John could
not even begin to number—washed their robes in
the blood of the Lamb (Revelation 7:9). That was the
ground of their access—they had been to Calvary.

Second, apart from the cross there is no assurance
of salvation either. It is a great privilege—the apex
of privilege says one theologian—to know that I
am a child of God. But how do I know I am a child
of God? Is it because I have a testimony to tell, a
life-changing experience to recount? Is it because I
have experienced spiritual highs and heavenly calms
that I can say I am a Christian? Is the extent of my
knowledge the thing that gives me assurance of
salvation?

No! Christ is all my assurance! The reason I know I
am a Christian is because, standing before the cross
of Calvary I can say of the Christ whose cross it is,
'This is my beloved, and this is my friend!' (Song of
Solomon 5:16).

In other words, if I am saved, and know God's life in
my soul and his Spirit in my life, then I too must keep
coming to the cross. I must keep surveying the cross,
in all its wonder and in all its power. Its attractiveness
does not diminish with the passage of time. It is what
assures me that there is no condemnation for me:
'Christ died' (Romans 8:35).

Where?
So I might ask the question: where do I survey the

cross? Where can I gaze on the cross? Where is it to
be seen? The answer to that question is that the cross
is to be seen in the Scriptures of the Old and the
New Testaments. This is the only vantage point from
which we can see the cross and gaze on its majesty
and glory. We survey the cross from the perspective
of the written word of Scripture. We allow the written
word to enable us to survey the wondrous Cross on
which the incarnate Word suffered and died.

Some of the books of the Bible were written prior to
the cross, and some were written afterwards. Even the
Gospels, the books that give us the historical facts of
what happened to Jesus, were written after the event,
not immediately at the time.

But the four Gospels do give us a fourfold account,
from different perspectives, on the events that led up
to Jesus being crucified. So, for a narrative of these
events, we turn to Matthew, Mark, Luke and John.

When we do, we notice immediately that these
books are not biographies of Jesus. That is to say, they
do not give us exhaustive, minute details of what
happened in Jesus' life. The writers are selective in
what they tell; John explicitly tells us that that had to
be so (John 20:30–31); and the reason they tell us what
they do is that we might believe in Jesus as the Son of
God.

In all four Gospels, however, there is a
disproportionate telling of the cross story; that is,
more space is devoted to the cross than to any other
aspect of Jesus' life and ministry. Time slows down

as the Gospel writers move towards the climax of their story. They want us to pause at the hours that Jesus suffered and bled at Calvary. There may be a clear selection of material, but that is matched with a definite focus of interest.

But even a reading of the Gospels points us in two directions. The opening words of Matthew's Gospel point us back to David and Abraham, and immediately ground the narrative in the prior events that make up the Old Testament. Indeed, throughout the Gospels, we are pointed back to what David said, and Isaiah, and Hosea, and Moses. All the prophets anticipated the cross and its work.

More than this, all the roads of the Old Testament, everything that God had ever said 'to the fathers by the prophets' (Hebrews 1:1) was with the cross in view. As the Spirit of Christ moved them, the prophets spoke of the sufferings of Christ and the subsequent glories (1 Peter 1:11). The cross is the centre, and the key, to the whole biblical narrative.

We can survey the cross, in other words, in the Old Testament just as much as in the Gospels. We can see it in Genesis, as God promises a victor who will crush Satan (Genesis 3:15). We can see it in Exodus, with the provision of a lamb-focussed redemption (Exodus 12). We can see it as we enter Leviticus with its prescription for sacrifices that had to be offered; and as we wade through the blood of animals slain on thousands of Jewish altars, we are reminded that there is no forgiveness of sins without bloodshed. And we wonder when it will all be over? We long for the last sacrifice to be offered, the last blood to be spilled. And Leviticus anticipates the cross; for it is the final sacrifice, after which, no more bloodshed is required.

We can see the cross in the Psalms, which explicitly speak about Jesus (for example, in Psalm 16 and Psalm 22). We can see it in the prophets, who speak about the suffering Messiah (for example in Isaiah 53). Indeed, without the witness of the Old Testament, our survey of the cross would be entirely incomplete.

But we need further teaching too. John, in recounting Jesus' teaching about the Holy Spirit in chapters 14-16 of his Gospel, anticipates a future recounting and experiencing of the power of the crucified Jesus. The apostles preach the cross in the Book of Acts, and Paul, Peter and John explain the cross in their New Testament letters.

We have no way to survey the cross except by the completed record of Scripture, the Bible, in all sixty-six books and in both Testaments. To survey the cross requires more than reading about it in the Gospels; it requires learning about it from every aspect of the Word of God.

Who?

So when we do that—when we survey the cross from the vantage point that the Bible gives—what do we see? There were many crosses, but they were not all wondrous. But the Bible invites us to look at a cross where we see a specific individual performing a specific task for a specific purpose. That is what makes Calvary's cross a 'wondrous' cross. It is not the place of crucifixion that gives wonder to the person who is dying on it. Indeed, the whole purpose of crucifixion was to rob the individual of every last fibre of dignity.

But there is a person who gives dignity to the cross. And who is this person? It is, in Isaac Watts' words, the Prince of Glory! Crosses were not designed for princes! They were designed for criminals—for lawbreakers, not for lawmakers. The wonder, however, of this cross is precisely the fact that it is no lawbreaker who hangs on it, but a lawmaker, a Prince—THE Prince of Glory.

The identity of the sufferer on the middle cross at Calvary is an interesting study. At one level we know that this particular cross is the death place of Jesus of Nazareth, the carpenter, whose mother was present to witness the agonising death of her son. This is a human death, and the human being who dies is the son of Mary and Joseph, in the prime of his vigour and manhood.

That is the truth, but it is not the whole truth. For the identity of the man on this cross is not something that can be deduced from his dying. It is something that has to be deduced from his own teaching, and from the subsequent teaching of the Bible. Who is the man of Calvary?

He is the one who was in the beginning with God (John 1:1). He is the one who existed before Abraham did (John 8:58). He is the one who came down from

Heaven (John 3:13; 6:38). He is the Son of Man—a title that identifies him with the supernatural figure of Daniel 7:13–14)—who *came* into this world for a purpose. He *came* to give his life (Mark 10:45). He *came* to seek and save the lost (Luke 19:10). He appeared for the purpose of salvation.

This Jesus who died at Calvary lived a human life, but his existence pre-dates his actual human existence in the world. He is the pre-existing Christ, the eternal word who 'became flesh and dwelt among us' (John 1:14).

Should such a One have been crucified? A thousand times NO! His life was without blemish, his conduct unimpeachable, his actions wholly justifiable. There was, in fact, no fault in the man, as Pilate so eloquently stated in John 18:38. The fault was in those who put him to death.

Paul states this categorically in 1 Corinthians 2, as he expounds the eternal purpose of God and says

> ... we impart a secret and hidden wisdom of God, which God decreed before the ages for our glory. None of the rulers of this age understood this, for if they had, they would not have crucified the Lord of glory' (1 Corinthians 2:7–8).

Paul's statement is staggering. The One who was crucified was the Lord of glory! It is a designation that James uses in James 2:1, where he talks of 'the faith in our Lord Jesus Christ, the Lord of glory'. So

Isaac Watts was right: the cross is the cross on which the *Prince of Glory* died. That is what makes the cross wondrous—not that it was a cross, but that it was this Person's cross.

Before we leave this point, let us just remind ourselves that if Jesus is the Prince of Glory, then he, and he alone, is the right object of all my worship and devotion. There is no other Lord of glory, but the One in whom all the fulness of the godhead dwells (Colossians 2:9). He is the Lord, the King of Glory (Psalm 24:7), the same 'God of glory' who appeared to Abraham (Acts 7:2). He is the great 'I am', and before him we humbly fall.

What?

But what is the reason that the Prince of glory turns the cross of Calvary into a *wondrous* cross? What happens at the cross to make it so compelling, so attractive and so central? In and of itself, a cross is not an attractive thing—it is repugnant and offensive, the kind of thing from which you would want to shield the eyes of your children.

In our popular mindset we have tamed the cross, and domesticated it in wood and silver and gold. We have conveniently removed the blood and gore, and silenced the screams of agony that accompanied this most cruel of all forms of execution.

Yet for us, as believers, the cross remains wondrous, and wonderfully attractive for one reason: on it, the Prince of glory *dies*. He actually 'dies'. He breathes his last breath there (Luke 23:46). He goes to the cross a living man, and is removed from it a dead man. And it is the combination of this person and this cross that makes atonement possible!

This is the whole reason for his coming into the world—to give his life as a ransom (Mark 10:45), to lay it down for his sheep (John 10:11). He comes into the world as a Servant, under compulsion to obey his Father, and it is the will of his Father to crush him (Isaiah 53:10).

For whom does Jesus die? Ultimately, he dies for his Father! God sent his Son into the world so that the world would be saved through him (John 3:17), and right up to the very last moment, the Prince of Glory yields to that will, saying 'Not my will, but your will be done' (Matthew 26:39). At Calvary, Jesus is honouring his Father, by laying down his life at the Father's command (John 10:18).

So it is the death of the Prince of Glory that makes the cross so wondrous. As one poet put it:

A crossless Christ my Saviour could not be,
A Christless cross no refuge is for me;
But, oh, Christ crucified! I rest in thee!

Why?
All of this arises out of the narrative of the Gospels: we know who is on this cross at the centre of the Bible story and we know what is happening to him.

But why does this happen to this person on this cross? Why does the Prince of Glory die?

I have never forgotten, and have often quoted, a line I read from the American theologian B. B. Warfield, who says that although Jesus died *on* the cross, he did not die *of* the cross. That is to say, although the cross was the means of his death, it was not the reason for it. Did Jesus die because he was crucified? No; he died because the sins of all of God's people in every place, and in every era of this world's history, were laid on him and charged to his account.

Jesus died because he stood before God as the representative of his people:

> Bearing shame and scoffing rude;
> In my place condemned he stood,
> Sealed my pardon with his blood;
> Hallelujah! What a Saviour![6]

I stand before that cross and I say to Jesus 'I am your sin—all the defects and blemishes and shortcomings and transgressions of my life are yours'. The Prince of Glory takes that burden and stands accountable for my sins as if they were his own. The sword of God's judgement and justice falls on him at Calvary. On that cross Jesus is at the judgement seat of God, and the whole weight of retributive justice falls with the penalty of a broken law like a torrent on his head. There, in that moment, he descends into hell, crying out 'My God, My God, why have you forsaken me?'

(Psalm 22:1). But because he does, he turns and says to me 'I am your righteousness—all the perfections of my life and death belong to you, my friend'.

What mind can fathom it? What eyes can look into it? This is beyond mystery—it is the place of substitutionary atonement, as the Prince of Glory, in my nature, stands accountable for my sin and lawbreaking. For, as I am his sin, he is my righteousness; the judge condemns him that he might spare me; condemns him that he might justify me.

This is the reason for his death—and the reason why we must survey the wondrous cross. It is no place for boasting or for self-congratulation; it is a place only for humble gratitude that the Son of God should love us and give himself for us (Galatians 2:20).

May God enable us to rejoice in the Saviour of his providing!

2

Sacrificing to the cross

... far be it from me to boast except in the cross of our Lord Jesus Christ, by which the world has been crucified to me, and I to the world.   *Galatians 6:14*

Forbid it Lord that I should boast
Save in the death of Christ my Lord
All the vain things that charm me most
I sacrifice them to his blood.

The Bible talks of the death of Jesus on the cross as a sacrifice. Unlike the sacrifices of the Old Testament, which had to be offered for sin on a regular recurring basis, the sacrifice of Christ was a once for all offering, unrepeated and unrepeatable. 'When Christ had offered for all time a single sacrifice for sins', says the letter to the Hebrews, 'he sat down at the right hand of God' (Hebrews 10:12).

Yet the death of Christ on the cross is a sacrifice that

demands a sacrifice, as Isaac Watts' hymn reminds us. How can we boast as we stand before the cross? This is Paul's argument in Romans 3, as he considers the nature of Christ's death on the cross. God put Christ forward, says Paul, 'as a propitiation by his blood, to be received by faith ... to show his righteousness at the present time, so that he might be just and the justifier of the one who has faith in Jesus' (Romans 3:24–26).

This is the heart of the atonement; this is what Jesus actually accomplished at the cross. He was the place where wrath and mercy met; where the righteous God kissed a guilty world. The anger of God against our sins was poured out on Jesus, so that we might be spared in God's mercy.

When we truly appreciate that fact—that God, in his love, provided a perfect Saviour and a perfect atonement, then we have nothing to say. We are silent before God, lost in wonder, love and praise.

Paul's great statement in Galatians 6 summarises the whole of his work and ministry and theology: 'Far be it from me to boast except in the cross of our Lord Jesus Christ'. In commenting on these words, Philip Ryken says, 'the cross is not just *something* to boast about, it is *the only thing* to boast about'.[7]

Boasting stops when we survey the cross. We have nothing in which to revel or to parade before God or anyone else. God's way of salvation leads to silence, 'so that every mouth may be stopped and the whole world may be held accountable to God' (Romans 3:19).

When I survey the cross, then I have no grounds for boasting at all; indeed, I ought to pour contempt on ALL my pride.

There are some things in which we *can* boast

There are things we have done, and places we have been, and things we have achieved, that fill us with satisfaction and self-congratulation, things in which we are inclined to boast. That works at different levels.

Some people boast about what they have.

Jeremiah captures this in his book:

> Let not the wise man boast in his wisdom, let not the mighty man boast in his might, let not the rich man boast in his riches, but let him that boasts boast in this, that he understands and knows me, that I am the LORD who practices steadfast love, justice and righteousness (Jeremiah 9:23–24).

These are the things that natural man wants to speak about—the extent of his knowledge, the greatness of his strength, and the wealth of his riches. The world is full of people for whom these are the great issues and goals of life. But Jeremiah pierces the bubble of such boasting; they are not worth boasting about.

The 'things that charm us most' are the things that will perish and decay, and very quickly disappear and

be gone. John Newton captured it too in the final
stanza of his great hymn, 'Glorious things of thee are
spoken':

> Saviour, if of Zion's city,
> I through grace a member am,
> Let the world deride or pity,
> I will glory in Thy Name.
> Fading is the worldling's pleasure,
> All his boasted pomp and show;
> Solid joys and lasting treasure
> None but Zion's children know.

The children of God know what is worth boasting
about: that they know God. Nothing else matters. For
this reason, John's counsel to the readers of his epistle
is clear:

> Do not love the world or the things in the world.
> If anyone loves the world, the love of the Father is
> not in him. For all that is in the world—the desires
> of the flesh and the desires of the eyes and pride of
> life—is not from the Father but is from the world. And
> the world is passing away along with its desires, but
> whoever does the will of God abides forever. (1 John
> 2:15–17)

There is a reason why the cross ought to be our only
ground of boasting: the effects of the cross alone are
eternal. Everything else vanishes away.

Some people boast about what they have been.
Paul took great pride in what he had been. This is how
he describes the ground of his belief that he was right
before God:

> If anyone else thinks he has reason for confidence
> in the flesh, I have more: circumcised on the eighth
> day, of the people of Israel, of the tribe of Benjamin,
> a Hebrew of Hebrews; as to the law, a Pharisee; as to
> zeal, a persecutor of the church; as to righteousness
> under the law, blameless. (Philippians 3:4–6).

Yet his discovery of the work of God in Christ made
him realise that nothing he had accomplished in his
good living or in his religion was adequate to make
him right with God:

> But whatever gain I had, I counted as loss for the sake
> of Christ. Indeed, I count everything as loss because of
> the surpassing worth of knowing Christ Jesus my Lord.
> For his sake I have suffered the loss of all things and
> count them as rubbish, in order that I may gain Christ
> and be found in him, not having a righteousness of my
> own that comes from the law, but that which comes
> through faith in Christ, the righteousness from God
> that depends on faith (Philippians 3:7–9).

The cross took away every reason he had for self-
satisfaction; to see what Jesus had done was to realise
that his 'plus' points were actually 'minus' points—his

good living was only taking him away from God, instead of drawing him to God. The only way in which he could be close to God was through trusting in the Lord Jesus Christ and his finished work.

Some people boast about what they have done.
Even those who know that the work of Christ is the only ground of our being right with God are apt to boast about what they have accomplished. Paul had to defend his ministry against those who were boasting in their achievements and in their accomplishments. That spirit was very far from Paul's own mind:

> We do not boast beyond limit in the labours of others. But our hope is that as your faith increases, our area of influence among you may be greatly enlarged, so that we may preach the gospel in lands beyond you, without boasting of work already done in another's area of influence. 'Let the one who boasts, boast in the Lord.' For it is not the one who commends himself who is approved, but the one whom the Lord commends. (2 Corinthians 10:15-18).

Indeed, as Paul goes on to explain, he too had reasons for boasting (2 Corinthians 10:21-28), but refused to make a show of his own greatness or his own achievements:
If I must boast, I will boast of the things that show my weakness. The God and Father of the Lord Jesus,

he who is blessed forever, knows that I am not lying. (2 Corinthians 10:30–31).

Paul goes on to describe his experiences of personal suffering, and of the way he discovered the all-sufficient help that God can give. That, at last, was the only reason he had to boast:

> ... he said to me, 'My grace is sufficient for you, for my power is made perfect in weakness.' Therefore I will boast all the more gladly of my weaknesses, so that the power of Christ may rest upon me. For the sake of Christ, then, I am content with weaknesses, insults, hardships, persecutions, and calamities. For when I am weak, then I am strong. (2 Corinthians 12:9–10).

There is only one thing in which we *must* boast
Paul knew that there was only one thing worth boasting in: 'far be it from me to boast except in the cross of our Lord Jesus Christ'. There was no ground for glorying in anything else. Only the finished work of Christ at Calvary was worth exulting in. For Paul, there were at least five reasons for that:

At the cross, God's Son was crucified
Paul looked at the cross, where the Prince of Glory died, and he was overwhelmed with the thought that all that was there was the evidence of God's love for an undeserving world. 'He loved me, and gave himself for me', he said in Galatians 2:20. The cross was not what secured God's love, but what expressed it. God

loved the world and gave his Son (John 3:16). Paul glories in the cross as the place where God himself stepped in to the curse; where he laid aside the crown of glory to wear a crown of thorns—a king still, but a king made a curse for his people.

The implication of that is radical. It means that there is nothing in me to which I can look or upon which I can rely for my salvation. All my salvation is outside of myself, and is concentrated on the cross. That is where I glory—in the place where salvation is actualised, not in me, but outside of me, and before me, on the wondrous cross.

At the cross, God's righteousness was magnified

The reason for this is not hard to find. There, at the cross, there is a righteousness that is not like a filthy rag: a law-keeping that is not compromised, and One with whom God is well pleased. All the requirements of God's holy law are exalted in Christ and by Christ. He does nothing but what is commanded, and omits nothing of what is required.

When I look at myself, I see nothing but UNrighteousness. When I look at him I see nothing but UNIrighteousness, all righteousness, one righteousness. His is one lawful, law-abiding, law-keeping life, where mine is one lawless, sinful life. I am all sin. But he is all righteousness.

Robert Murray McCheyne wrote his great hymn 'Jehovah Tsidkenu, The Lord our Righteousness' in November 1834. He had not yet been licensed to preach, but he had been laid low with one of the fevers which was to plague his short life. 'McCheyne's awareness of death and his own frailty', writes one of his biographers, 'was to be a characteristic of his ministry'.[8]

And out of that recognition of the frailty and uncertainty of human life came these great words:

> When free grace awoke me, by light from on high,
> Then legal fears shook me, I trembled to die;
> No refuge, no safety in self could I see—
> Jehovah Tsidkenu my Saviour must be.

That is the point—*no refuge, no safety in self.* For refuge and safety, a sinner must go outside self, and must flee to Jesus Christ. Only in him is the righteousness of God manifested apart from the law, 'the righteousness of God through faith in Jesus Christ'.

At the cross, God's justice was satisfied

There could be no salvation unless God, as the judge of all the earth, was satisfied that the right thing had been done with respect to sin. After all, although it is true that 'The LORD is slow to anger and abounding in steadfast love, forgiving iniquity and transgression,' it is also true that 'he will by no means clear the guilty', but will visit the iniquity of the fathers on the children (Numbers 14:18).

Yet the glory of the gospel is that iniquities can be

cleared, and sins can be forgiven. The only reason for this is that God is satisfied that the penalty has been paid, that sin's debt has been cleared, and that all that the law demanded as a punishment for sin has been carried out.

The wonder and beauty of the cross is that this was done through substititution:

> Bearing sin and scoffing rude;
> 'In my place condemned he stood
> Sealed my pardon with his blood:
> Hallelujah! What a Saviour!'

When Jesus dies on behalf of his people, taking their place and their punishment, God was pleased; not in the sense that the death of his Son gave him *pleasure*, but that it gave him *satisfaction*. There was no compromise to the highest standards of justice and right. Justice was done when Jesus took the place of his people.

At the cross, God's wrath was pacified

As a consequence, the anger of God, of which the Bible speaks frequently (Psalm 2:12; Romans 1:18; Hebrews 12:29; Revelation 6:16), was poured out and consumed Jesus Christ. It cannot be recalled and poured out again a second time. In fact, the position of the Christian is precisely that of the prophet Isaiah when he said

> I will give thanks to you, O Lord,
> for though you were angry with me,
> your anger turned away,
> that you might comfort me (Isaiah 12:1).

The cross did not turn God's anger into love. The love and the anger of God reside in the same heart. But in love he provided a substitute, upon whom his wrath was poured, so that love, and not anger, might reach a guilty world. This is simply the New Testament doctrine of *propitiation*: Christ was made like his brothers in order that he might be a faithful high priest, to make propitiation for our sins (Hebrews 2:17). God is angry with him at Calvary, and, like the lightning conductor that takes the full force of the lightning strike to save the church steeple, he is struck that I might be comforted.

At the cross, God's people are justified
The end result of this is that all who are in Christ Jesus are justified. They still sin, and mourn for their sin; they are not what they ought to be, nor what they try to be; they glory only in the cross, where Christ was delivered that they might be set free. Paul states it categorically when he says that 'we have now been justified by his blood' (Romans 5:9), and declared to be not guilty, and under no more condemnation.

Little wonder, then, that this is a wondrous cross, apart from which we have no reason to boast, and no grounds for satisfaction. Are we trusting to this cross alone as the basis of our hope and all our salvation?

There is only one way to show that we are boasting in the cross

'All the vain things that charm me most I sacrifice them to his blood'. At the wondrous cross my great high priest offered up the great sacrifice for sins, one sacrifice for all the sins of all his people for all of time and for the whole of eternity. Even in Heaven they boast in the cross as they sing the praises of him who loved them and freed them from their sins by his blood (Revelation 1:5). Nothing matters but the cross.

And how do we show that the cross matters? By taking the things that charmed us and sacrificing them to the cross of Calvary. I take my abilities and strengths, my experience and my knowledge, my righteousnesses and my good works, and I place them before his cross, counting them as nothing that I might be found in him (Philippians 3:9). I take my silver and my gold, and I sacrifice them to his cross that they might be for him. I take my days and weeks and years and I yield them to him, presenting myself as a living sacrifice to him who gave himself as a sacrifice for me (Romans 12:1).

If my salvation is in the cross, then my life must take the shape of the cross. It must be *cruciform* if it is *crucicentric*. If the cross is at the centre, the cross must mould my life and conform it to its own shape. Jesus does not save us by being a moral example to us; he saves us by suffering and dying on our behalf. But having done that, his cross becomes exemplary; it becomes the standard of our lives:

> ... to this you have been called, because Christ also suffered for you, leaving you an example, so that you might follow in his steps. He committed no sin, neither was deceit found in his mouth. When he was reviled, he did not revile in return; when he suffered, he did not threaten, but continued entrusting himself to him who judges justly. He himself bore our sins in his body on the tree, that we might die to sin and live to righteousness (1 Peter 2:21–24).

The wonder of the cross means that it does not matter what you have done before: you may come to the Saviour's blood and righteousness and find life. But it also means that, having come, it matters what you do now. Have you sacrificed your vain things to the cross where Christ, the passover lamb, was sacrificed for us?

3

The suffering of the cross

So Jesus came out, wearing the crown of thorns and the purple robe. Pilate said to them, 'Behold the Man!'   John 19:5

See from his head, his hands, his feet
Sorrow and love flow mingled down;
Did e'er such love and sorrow meet?
Or thorns compose so rich a crown?

The cross of Jesus was a place of suffering and pain. It could not be otherwise. The design of the cross was to maximise the pain of the crucified one. There is perhaps nothing that symbolises the suffering of Jesus quite like the crown of thorns. Plaited in order to mock Jesus' claim to kingship, along with the purple robe and the reed that was placed in his hand, the crown only served to show how much Jesus was willing to endure on behalf of his people. In Isaac Watts' words, this was a place where love and sorrow met, and where they met as unparalleled, extraordinary realities in the experience of the Lord Jesus Christ.

When Handel's great oratorio, *The Messiah*, was performed in London in the 1780s, John Newton was minister of St Mary Woolnoth. He preached—perhaps as an evangelistic opportunity—a series of fifty expository sermons on the passages from the Bible which form the text of Handel's work. One of these is Isaiah 50:6—'I gave my back to the smiters and my cheeks to them that plucked off the hair: I hid not my face from shame and spitting' (AV).

Newton entitled this sermon 'Voluntary Suffering', noting the twin emphases of the text, that in all that he suffered Christ 'gave' himself and did not hide his face; and that in all he suffered he suffered in the extreme—he gave his back and his cheeks to shame, smiting and spitting. Of the first of these, Newton says

'With respect to his engagement, as the Mediator between God and sinners, a great work was given him to do, and he became responsible; and therefore, in this sense, bound, and under obligation. But his compliance was likewise *voluntary*, for he gave himself up freely to suffer … if he was determined to save others, then his own sufferings were unavoidable'.[9]

Newton goes on:

'He knew that no blood but his own could make

atonement for sin; that nothing less than his
humiliation could expiate our pride; that if he did
not thus suffer, sinners must inevitably perish;
and therefore (such was his love) he cheerfully and
voluntarily gave his back to the smiters ...'[10]

That is the thought before us—Jesus 'cheerfully and
voluntarily' giving himself over to the cruel torment
of his persecutors and of the cross, being willing, out
of love, to wear a crown of thorns and suffer for his
people. These voluntary sufferings make the cross a
wondrous one, and the crown a rich one. From every
part of the Saviour's body—from his head, his hands
and his feet, sorrow and love flow mingled down.

Christ's loving suffering
Let's focus for a moment on this crown that he wore.
Christ's tormentors wove it out of thorns in order
to mock his claim to be a king. It was not placed
on his head in order to dignify him, but in order to
degrade him. He has been made, in the words of F.
W. Krummacher, 'a carnival king'.[11] And although we
know that he does not wear a crown of thorns now
but the dignity of a name above all other names,
'He left us his thorn-crowned image in the gospel,
and oh, the wonders it has wrought in the world,
and continues to perform, whenever the Holy Spirit
illumines it!'[12]

So let's study this thorn-crowned image. What is it
saying to us?

It was a measure, first, *of the hardness of the sinful heart.*

It was to wicked people that Jesus gave his head, his hands and his feet. He came to save a guilty, sinful world, who repaid all his compassion, his miracles, his kindness, his love and his grace with the judgement 'We will not have this man to reign over us'. They were masters of their own destiny and of their own lives. The mock crown that was put on Jesus' head was only symbolic of the fact that the actual crown was placed on their own. The crown of authority and rule they relegated to themselves; for the Lord of glory they made a garland of thorns.

The heart of man still responds this way to Jesus. The cross becomes the symbol of a rejected Jesus by hearts that have become their own master. Everyone is placing a crown on Jesus' head—either a crown of golden sovereignty, by which they are acknowledging him as king of their lives, or a crown of thorns, by which they are crucifying 'once again the Son of God to their own harm and holding him up to contempt' (Hebrews 6:6). The crown of thorns was a reminder that Jesus was suffering at the hands of men.

It was a measure, secondly, *of the physical pain of Calvary.*

One could not wear a crown of thorns without getting hurt. That was the design of the object. Pressed into his brow, it inflicted injury, pain and distress in one of the most sensitive parts of the body.

It is impossible to overstate the pain of the cross.

So agonising was it that we have our own word in English that derives from it—the word 'excruciating'. Jesus was subjected to physical abuse and torture even before he was impaled on the cross, with nails driven through his hands and feet. And the cross itself inflicted its own pain as the victim struggled to breathe and gradually died as his lungs filled with water. None of us can measure the depth of that pain.

If there had been any other way to save us, God would have saved us that way. He was free to save us or not to save us. He could have left us to perish. He could have made us suffer what Christ suffered. There was no obligation on God's part to be merciful to us.

But the moment he opted to be gracious, to reach into the pit of sin and pluck sinners out of the fire, rescuing them from sin's power and sin's punishment, he was not free to decide the way that should be done. Only one way was possible—the way of pain, of suffering and of death. That is why B. B. Warfield is correct to remind us that 'The theology of the writers of the New Testament is very distinctly a "blood theology"' (in his *Works*, Volume 2, Chapter 9, 'Christ our sacrifice'). Without the shedding of blood there is no forgiveness of sins (Hebrews 9:22).

So the blood that flows from Immanuel's veins is not simply an accident of the instruments used to torture him; the bloodshed is the design of these instruments—they are a means to that end. The cross, with all its suffering and agony, was the means of Christ's death, but not the reason for it. The reason was that he was giving himself for us, in the totality of our need and guilt, in order that we might be set free. The Son of God loved his church, and gave himself for her (Ephesians 5:25).

Third, *it reminds us of the curse of God for our sin.*

Can we look at these thorns, plaited into a mock crown, and not think of the words which God said to man following his sin:

'Cursed is the ground because of you; in pain you shall eat of it all the days of your life; thorns and thistles it shall bring forth for you ...' (Genesis 3:17–18).

The ground which man was given to work, and which supplied all his needs so magnificently, was now under a curse, which would leave it groaning and in pain (Romans 8:22). The very place which was the theatre of God's glory was to bear the legacy of man's rebellion; where once 'the earth brought forth vegetation, plants yielding seed according to their own kinds, and trees bearing fruit in which is their seed, according to its kind; and God saw that it was good' (Genesis 1:12)—now there would be thorns and thistles.

The presence of the thorns was a powerful symbol of that curse. And now, Jesus is crowned with the symbols of the curse. The language of the curse is precisely how Paul describes the atonement:

'Christ redeemed us from the curse of the law by becoming a curse for us ... so that in Christ Jesus the

blessing of Abraham might come to the Gentiles, so
that we might receive the promised Spirit through
faith' (Galatians 3:13–14).

Here then is a fundamental aspect of the New
Testament doctrine of the atonement—there is
blessing for us because there was cursing for him. We
will receive a crown of righteousness because he wore
a crown of thorns. He was the great benefactor—
the one who did good—who suffered between the
malefactors—the ones who did evil. But in order
to benefit them with his benediction, he had to
experience the malediction, the curse of God on him
for our sins.

So that at last Christ redeems us by appearing before
God, stripped naked apart from his cursed crown;
and with no comfort except the knowledge that he
was doing the will of his Father. This was the loving
suffering that he was willing to endure—mocking,
scourging, crucifixion, isolation, banishment,
forsakenness; and it was all for us: damnation, taken
lovingly. Professor T. F. Torrance expresses it like this:

> 'At last the hour had come when Christ was to
> make atonement, at last the king of truth in vicarious
> suffering stormed into the ultimate stronghold of sin
> embattled and embittered by sheer resentment to
> grace, and expiated it in unutterable compassion and at
> unheard of cost'.[13]

Christ's suffering love

Did every such sorrow flow from the body of such a man? Yet it was not in order to show us the limit of human endurance or the capacity of the human body for suffering that Christ experienced the anguish of the cross. It was to show us the extent of his love. His body was racked with pain even as his heart was full of love.

The cross demonstrated on the one hand *Christ's love for his Father*. It was explicitly to show this that he left the upper room: '... I do as the Father commanded me, so that the world may know that I love the Father' (John 14:31).

That love was eternal, as the Father and the Son existed in the fellowship of divine love that is the life of God. Jesus came down from Heaven to do the will of the Father who had sent him (John 6:37), and to finish his work.

It is impossible to do justice to what happened at Calvary unless we see it in the context of an engagement between God the Father and God the Son. Some theologians refer to this as a 'covenant of redemption', the engagement by which the Son of God, who is the Father's equal and is one with him, comes to be the Father's Servant, and subordinate to him.

All he suffers he suffers within this context of love. The Father says 'This is my Son' (Matthew 17:5), but he also says 'Behold my Servant!' (Isaiah 42:1). Although in all things Christ was in the form of God, he took the form of a servant in addition (Philippians 2:7). There was never such love to God as there was displayed on Calvary's cross.

But on the other hand, the cross demonstrated *Christ's love for sinners*. All through his life and ministry he had been showing his love for others, in gifts of compassion and ministries of mercy. But nowhere did he show his love more powerfully or magnificently than when he died at Calvary for them. By his own admission, 'greater love has no one than this, that someone lay down his life for his friends' (John 15:12).

The love of Christ for his own people is what causes them to view the cross in wonder and amazement. 'Did e'er such love and sorrow meet?'. Was there ever such a combination of unmerited love and undeserved sorrow? He did not deserve what was done to him; I certainly did not deserve what was done for me. He was willing to enter the pain and agony of abandonment and forsakenness precisely so that I might be set free, and might know the blessing of God's salvation and his redeeming grace in my life.

In discussing this theme, John Bunyan writes:

'The love of Christ appears to be wonderful by the death he died, in that *he* died, in that he died *such* a death. 'Twas strange love in Christ that moved him to die for us; strange, because not according to the custom of the world. Men do not use, in cold blood, deliberately to come upon the stage or ladder, to lay down their lives for others; but this did Jesus Christ, and that too for such, whose qualification, if it be duly considered, will make this act of his far more amazing: he laid down his life for his enemies, and for those that could not abide him, yea, for those, even for those that brought him to the cross: not accidentally, or because it happened so, but knowingly, designedly ... he knew it was for those he died, and yet his love led him to lay down his life for them'.[14]

No wonder John writes that 'we love because he first loved us' (1 John 4:19).

Faith's view of the cross

All of this is what makes the cross supremely attractive to the eye of faith. 'See!' said Isaac Watts—behold the man! He is there for us, doing what we could never do for ourselves, and securing redemption and salvation for his own. Faith can never get enough of him. Faith wants to know the love of Christ which passes knowledge (Ephesians 3:19). It desires to be found in him alone (Philippians 3:9). And it draws all its strength and comfort from looking away from self to him, who bled and died. The hymn writer had it right:

Before the throne of God above
I have a strong, a perfect plea;
A great high priest whose name is love,
Who ever lives and pleads for me.[15]

Faith can be content with nothing less.

4

Surrendering to the cross

Do you see this woman? I entered your house; you gave me no water for my feet, but she has wet my feet with her tears and wiped them with her hair. You gave me no kiss, but from the time I came in she has not ceased to kiss my feet. You did not anoint my head with oil, but she has anointed my feet with ointment. Therefore I tell you, her sins, which are many, are forgiven—for she loved much.   *Luke 7:44–47*
What shall I render to the Lord for all his benefits to me?   *Psalm 116:12*

Were the whole realm of nature mine
That were a present far too small.
Love so amazing, so divine,
Demands my soul, my life, my all.

We have been surveying the cross of Jesus, and glorying in all that it represented as the place of atonement where Jesus suffered for the forgiveness of our sins. On it our representative and substitute poured out his soul to death, so that we would be healed with his stripes (Isaiah 53:6). His willing suffering is the result of his great love for his people.

We survey that cross from the vantage point of the whole realm of Scripture, and we marvel that such love and such sorrow should combine in one life and in one moment of time. Yet that is the nature of Calvary's great transaction: my sins are laid on the substitute, and his righteousness is given over to me. This was a wondrous cross, on which a wonderful Saviour completed a wonderful work for all of his people.

And it simply begs the question—how shall I respond to it? What will I give to the Christ who gave his all for me? To use the words of the Psalmist, 'What shall I render to the Lord for all his benefits to me?' (Psalm 116:12).

At one level, of course, there is nothing I can give. I did not merit the cross, or deserve it, or earn it. It was not any labour of my hands that could fulfill the law's demands. No work of mine could have done what his work did, and no offering of mine is an adequate payment for it. To quote from Isaac Watts, 'Were the whole realm of nature mine, that were a present far too small'. Could I give everything I possess, it would be an inadequate and poor response to what Christ gave for me. And supposing I owned everything, and was prepared to give that away, it still would not do justice to what Christ did for me at Calvary.

So how shall I respond to the cross? How does faith respond to the man of Calvary and his dying love and loving dying? What will we do with the Prince of Glory? What will we give? In the cross we have every spiritual blessing in heavenly places in Christ Jesus, and all we have is at the discretion of God's grace and mercy. So what does faith do in response to the work of Jesus Christ?

Faith responds by receiving *from* Jesus
By definition, a Christian is someone who has received from Christ. It is not what we have done that makes us Christians; it is what Christ has done that makes us Christians. It is not the labour of our hands, or our zeal or goodness that have secured us peace with God; if we have our sins forgiven and we have peace with God, it is because we have received what Jesus offers in the gospel.

Faith is about the only grace that does nothing. We can do many things through faith; if we want to do the best things in the best way we must do them by faith. But faith in its very essence and kernel does nothing because by definition it is a receiving grace. The beggar on the street is enriched not because he earns the money he has, but because he has begged for it. Rich people have put money into the outstretched hand of the beggar.

Faith is the same—it is a hand stretched out towards

Jesus, to take what he gives. Peace in my conscience, and the joy of God in my soul, and the presence of the Holy Spirit in my life are all *received* blessings. I could not have them unless I was a Christian; but nor could I ever earn them. They are blessings to be received by faith.

Faith, in other words, responds to the offer of the gospel, and receives the Christ that is offered. Paul's argument in Romans 4 is that salvation depends on faith that it might rest on grace: it is faith that highlights that salvation is all of grace and that God's grace is the source of all these blessings.

It is important to distinguish the source of salvation from the method of salvation: God's grace, that alone saves, saves in a particular way. The God who alone elects and comes down in sovereign grace to save sinners has appointed a particular method by which he does that—he offers Jesus. He has an open invitation to sinners to come to him. The glory of the gospel is seen in this very fact.

John Flavel, one of the great Puritans, has a series of sermons on this very topic: 'the method of grace in gospel redemption'. What is this method? Flavel preaches on John 1:12 and highlights the word 'received' ... 'to as many as received him, he gave power to be called the sons of God'.

Have we received Christ? That is the great question, not whether we are good enough for God, but whether God is good enough for us! Will we take the Jesus who is offered in the gospel?

Flavel probes this idea of Christ being offered in the gospel. How is he offered, he asks? Well, he says, he is offered *sincerely*. This is an invitation that comes sincerely from God. If you follow the terms of the invitation you will get what is offered. The opportunity for salvation comes in the gospel, and it is a sincere offer.

Flavel says that Christ is offered *entirely*; it is not a part Christ we get when we believe, but a whole Christ. We get the Christ of Calvary with the majesty of his finished work. We get the Christ in whom all our sins are washed away. We get the Christ who makes us holy and prepares us for glory. We get the prophet Christ who teaches us, the priest Christ who intercedes, the king Christ to reign over us and protect us. Christ is offered to us wholly.

Third, Flavel says that Christ is offered *exclusively*. He does not give his glory to anyone else. There is no-one else. Christ alone is offered in the gospel. He is there for the taking, and there is no other Saviour on offer.

Fourth, he is offered to us *freely*. We don't need to make ourselves ready to come to him, we simply come as sinners to receive him as a gift. Our lives do not need to be reformed or well-groomed; Jesus came for vile, guilty, lost, hell-deserving sinners and offers himself to us. The gospel, says Flavel, is God's gift, not God's sale. Heaven is not offered us with a 50% discount; it is offered to us in Christ absolutely freely.

Fifth, Christ is offered to us *advisedly*. Flavel pictures

the soul wondering what to do with the great issues of Heaven and Hell, with guilt and with sin, and then Christ is offered in such a way as to convince the troubled, peace-less soul that the only way to find peace is to take Christ.

So faith answers its own question: What shall I render to the Lord for his benefits to me? I will *take* the cup of salvation (Psalm 116:12–13). There is nothing I can render; I can only take the Christ who invites me to come to him. Sinclair Ferguson puts it like this: 'It is of the nature of faith that by it we actively receive Christ and justification in him without contributing to it. After all, faith is trust in another. It is the antithesis of all self-contribution and self-reliance'[16]

I was recently reading the epitaph on the grave of John Wesley. It is an elaborate celebration of Wesley's work and ministry:

To the Memory of
THE VENERABLE JOHN WESLEY. A.M.
Late Fellow of Lincoln College. Oxford.
This GREAT LIGHT arose
(By the singular Providence of GOD)
To enlighten THESE NATIONS,
And to revive, enforce, and defend,
The Pure Apostolic DOCTRINES and PRACTICES of
THE PRIMITIVE CHURCH:
Which he continued to do, both by his WRITINGS and his
LABOURS

For more than HALF A CENTURY:
And to his inexpressible Joy,
Not only, beheld their INFLUENCE extending,
And their EFFICACY witness'd
In the Hearts and Lives of MANY THOUSANDS,
As well in THE WESTERN WORLD as in THESE KINGDOMS:
But also, far above all human Power of Expectation,
Liv'd to see PROVISION made by the singular Grace of GOD,
For their CONTINUANCE and ESTABLISHMENT,
TO THE JOY OF FUTURE GENERATIONS
READER if thou art contrain'd to bless the INSTRUMENT,
GIVE GOD THE GLORY.
After having languished a few Days, He at length finished his
COURSE and his LIFE together. Gloriously triumphing over
DEATH March 2nd An. Dom. 1791 in the Eighty eighth Year of
his Age.

Yet when he was fifty, John Wesley took ill. He was
so ill he didn't know if he would survive the day, so he
thought he'd better write his own epitaph, just in case
he died and had to be buried, and to prevent anyone
writing what he called a 'vile panegyric'. In other
words, he did not want a eulogy that simply praised
his achievements. He would not have been pleased
with what went on his gravestone. This is what he
wrote for himself:

Here lieth the body of John Wesley
A brand plucked out of the burning
who died of a consumption in the fifty-first year of his

age
not leaving, after his debts are paid, ten pounds behind
him
praying, God be merciful to me, an unprofitable
servant.

When he died, people wanted to talk about everything he'd done, to write on his gravestone how he was a bright light to the nations; but all that mattered to him was that he, as a poor sinner, could pray to a great God for mercy and for salvation. Christ completed all that was necessary for the salvation of Wesley's soul; Wesley simply wanted to receive that salvation by faith.

Faith responds by trusting *in* Jesus

What will we render to Christ in response to all that the Prince of Glory did for us? What can we do but continue to trust in him? The grace that saves is the grace that keeps; the grace that enabled us to receive him is the grace that we need at every point along life's way.

We do not know about the future; our lives may change in a moment. One decision can turn everything around; one day can make the rest of our lives altogether different to what we had planned. It does not take much for our plans to be altered beyond recognition. Every day we die a thousand deaths grieving for the things we thought we would do or thought we would have.

But because of what the Prince of Glory did for us on that wondrous cross it is possible for us to have the assurance that whatever comes our way, his grace will be enough for us (2 Corinthians 12:9). The Prince of Glory is the Prince of Grace too.

Christ wants us simply to keep trusting in him. We have a great high priest in the Heavens (Hebrews 4:14), but we do not have a priest who does not know our weaknesses. He knows about living in a fallen world, and how to face temptation and difficulty. He walked this way before us, and knows our frame (Psalm 103:14). So we may come to him for mercy and grace.

John Newton expressed it beautifully in one of his great hymns:

Approach my soul the mercy seat
Where Jesus answers prayer;
There humbly fall before His feet,
For none can perish there.

Thy promise is my only plea,
With this I venture nigh;
Thou callest burdened souls to Thee,
And such, O Lord, am I.

Bowed down beneath a load of sin,
By Satan sorely pressed,
By war without and fears within,
I come to Thee for rest.

Be Thou my Shield and hiding Place,
That, sheltered near Thy side,
I may my fierce accuser face,
And tell him Thou hast died!

O wondrous love! to bleed and die,
To bear the cross and shame,
That guilty sinners, such as I,
Might plead Thy gracious Name.

'Poor tempest-tossèd soul, be still;
My promised grace receive';
'Tis Jesus speaks—I must, I will,
I can, I do believe.

Do we realise that the Jesus of Calvary says 'My promised grace receive' just as surely as he says 'Receive my salvation'.

Faith responds by living *for* Jesus

There is nothing we can do to earn our salvation. The primary action of faith is to take, to receive what is offered in the gospel.

But there is a reflex action of faith. Once we have seen the wonder of the cross, and the glory of his climactic 'it is finished', we know that the world would be an offering far to small to give him in response; but we also want to say 'Love so amazing, so divine, demands my soul, my life, my ALL'.

'Do you see this woman?' said Jesus to Simon in

Luke 7—a woman of whom Simon was wondering how Jesus could let her near him—'she was forgiven much'. It is possible to be forgiven much; for the blood of Calvary to wash away many sins. And because she was forgiven much, she loved much. She knew that love so amazing as to send a Saviour into the world who was willing to live, and suffer and die and conquer death for her, just as if no-one else mattered at all, that love deserves all her glad, willing response in service to him.

C. T. Studd had it right when he said that 'if Christ be God and died for me, then no sacrifice is too great for me to make for him'. How does faith respond to Jesus? Faith says 'To do your will I take delight' (Psalm 40:6). Faith wants to follow in the footsteps of this great Jesus, to live as he lived, to serve as he served, to die with all the humble resignation to the will of the Father that marked out Jesus' death as it had marked out the whole of his life.

Is that our song? There is something wrong if we can survey the cross and remember with gratitude the dying love of a gracious Saviour and then go out and live as we pleased, as if it mattered nothing.

Has this cross moulded and shaped our lives, so that people see how we live, and what we choose and what we aim for, and recognise it as a Christ-honouring, Christ-serving life? Does our life go against the stream? Do they see us serving him with our tears and the hair of our head? Does the world know that we love Jesus? Does the world recognise that there is only one passion in our lives—to live with a Jesus obsession.

That is why the disciples were called 'Christians' in Antioch, because it was so evident that they were Christ's ones, obsessed with him. Do people know our obsession? Can they see it on our Facebook pages, our tweets, our conversations, our lifestyles? Can they tell that our faith is not simply crucicentric—centred on the cross—but cruciform—shaped like a cross, because we have taken our cross and deny ourselves to live for him. Will we tell them about the things God has done for us?

Are you a Christian? If not, then you must take him in the gospel; your choice is either to have him and be in union with him here, or be separated from him throughout eternity. If so, are you living in dependence on him and obedience to him? Are you ready to die tonight? And if it is not God's will that you die tonight, are you ready to live for him and serve him every day of your life?

God forbid that we should glory in anything except the cross, which demands our all.

Notes

1   Kenneth W. Osbeck, *Amazing Grace*: 366 Inspiring Hymn Stories for Daily Devotions, Kregel Publications, 1990, p. 106

2   Faith Cook, *Our Hymn Writers and their Hymns*, Evangelical Press, 2005, p. 59

3   David Fountain, *Isaac Watts Remembered 1674–1748*, Mayflower Christian Bookshop, 1998, p. 38

4   Fountain, *Isaac Watts Remembered*, p. 7

5   Quoted in Fountain, *Isaac Watts Remembered*, p. 58

6   Philip P. Bliss

7   P. Ryken, *Galatians*, Reformed Expository Commentary, P&R publishing, Phillipsburg, New Jersey, 2005, p. 275

8   David Robertson, *Awakening*, Authentic Media, 2004, p. 40

9   *The Works of John Newton*, Volume 4, Banner of Truth, 2007, pp. 211–12

10   Newton Volume 4, p. 212

11   F.W. Krummacher, *The Suffering Saviour*, Kregel Publications, 1992, p. 282

12   Krummacher, p. 287

13   Thomas F. Torrance, *Incarnation: The Person and Work of Christ*, IVP, 2008, p. 156

14   Works of John Bunyan, Volume 2, p. 17

15   Charitie L. Bancroft

16   Sinclair B. Ferguson, *The Holy Spirit*, IVP, 1996, p. 128